the Deepy

from France

KENNETH PUA & ANDY KUNZ

Copyright © 2017 Kenneth Pua & Andy Kunz

ISBN: 978 1976 729 478

All rights are reserved and any reproduction of/and copying from the book whether through mechanical or digital means for commercial is strictly prohibited. However part(s) of this book may be reproduced and/or copied without written permission for articles, review and/or further studies with special mention of the source.

Printed in the United States of America

INTRODUCTION

Everyone in the martial arts community likes the feeling of walking the mean streets, confident that he will be able to defend himself when the need arise. However that kind of feeling can be dangerous when you found out on the dark alley that you're wrong. Always keep in mind that it didn't take 10 or  more years for the crack head on the street who will assault you. The muggers just did his fighting techniques the practical way, by mugging and assaulting experience.

Realistic experience is the key to realistic self-defense techniques. Realistic self-defense comes from spontaneous reactions, based on solid foundations of the basic human kinetics principle.

One good concept for realistic self-defense is the principle of nonresistance, and the integration of a counter attack as your defense. When an attacker executes a strike whether a kick/punch/grab, you don't block. You just move away from the line of attack and strike back at the same time. Facts should rule all self-defense or fighting tactics. To be able to strike with power is to strike with explosion of the hip rotation, incorporation of body weight to the strike and the acceleration of the strike whether it is a kick or a punch.

Two most important part of realistic self-defense training is timing and distancing. Practical training will teach you when to attack and how to close the striking distance. Distancing is affected by intention. Self-defense techniques and strategies you need to develop are the punching, kicking range, close quarter, grappling, and various street weapons range.

Possible weapons you will encounter on the streets are bladed weapon, broken bottle glass, baseball bat, improvised knife, and many more.

No self-defense techniques will work unless you did them right and experience them first hand. Those who say that the best kick in a street fight is a side kick to the groin or knee, should practice sidekicks to knee or groin of a simulation target. The only way to learn if you're doing it right is to practice with an unwilling partner, who would resist you. So I suggest you select a partner at your gym that you hate most and also hate you.

Joinville Military Academy – France.

For you to have a realistic experience as much as possible. In realistic self-defense the human body is your weapon and the body of the attacker is the opening and the target. Realism says there is no such thing as creating an opening for you to strike. In that sense, everything is your target – the attacker's heel, elbow, head, neck, wrist, and others.

Like all martial arts Savate has undergone innumerable changes over time to adapt it to the needs of a given period. When used by the hardscrabble sailors of Toulon, Marseilles, Algiers and La Havre it took into account the use of the ropes and rigging found on tall ships to aid in wild looping boot-strikes delivered with a cutlass in one hand. The bold highwaymen of the vast French interior adapted it to their own needs when plundering coaches with a knife and pistol at their side. Just before the turn of the 19th century in Paris it had become a polite exercise in gymnastics for the bourgeoisie and idle noblemen. But things had changed in the capital, and the members of the upper crust were no longer in command of the streets as desperate young men formed street gangs such as the "Apaches" to rob and terrorize the moneyed classes.

Apaches (French: [a.paʃ]) was a Parisian Belle Époque violent criminal underworld subculture of hooligans, night muggers, street gangs and other criminals.

The Apaches also evolved a semi-codified collection of "tricks" used in mugging and hand-to-hand combat. A prospective victim will be stalked by several Apaches. One will garrote the victim from behind while taking him piggyback to prevent the victim from struggling; then another Apache will be assigned the job of searching through the victim's pockets for any valuables, and another one will

served as a lookout. Although only meant to

incapacitate, the chance of death from prolonged strangulation do happen.

During their heyday, the prospect of being mugged or otherwise assaulted by Apache gangsters was especially feared by members of the emergent bourgeois (Upper Class of the Victorian Era French Society).

A 1904 issue of the French question-and-answer magazine *L'Intermédiaire des chercheurs et curieux* credited a journalist named Victor Moris with the popularization of the term. In November 1900 a police inspector of the Belleville district of police was describing to him a particularly bloody scene and concluded with the words: "C'est un véritable truc d'Apaches!

The Apache is the sore of Paris. More than 30,000 prowlers against 8,000 city policemen

A story in a 1910 Sunday supplement of *Le Petit Journal* claimed that when a certain gang leader nicknamed *Terreur* (Terror) heard that the actions of the band were compared with these of the Apaches, he was so pleased that he proceeded to call his gang "Apaches of Belleville"

EARLY RECORD

If Pugilism is a word of modern origin, the year it represents is as old as the beginning of man. Not to mention the struggle that early Man had, in principle, the survival against elements and animals. And the struggle daily with his fellow mankind for survival. Where the resolution for survival is through brute force. **To Quote Hobbes-** *Homo Homini lupus – Man is a wolf to man.*

Man had to defend and protect himself, and that offensive and defensive weapons did not exist at that time. And that man is forced to use the easiest and most natural weapon available to him his hands, foot, teeth and head. Indeed these are the only ones that are always available for his disposal and for his defense. Also from the earliest of times, man engages in a violent exercises that a relax muscles was nonexistent, this hardened type of ballistic approach cause fatigue and cause the struggle for existence of self-inflicted injuries. And early history teaches us that societies in the past was open to all for the taking, And the child learns survival the hard way. Ancient Greek history taught us that the ancient fighting ground was open to all, the women went there at times to send their children to be trained as fighters, as we send our child to school today.

It now remain to say a few words about Savate, the origins are neither very noble nor very old; it was born, in fact when the shoe was used by man, At a time when shoe became fashionable among men of the world, Savate came to existence and its development. In the earlier time .To get a lessons of Savate. One needs to train in the back room of a wine merchant or the back alley, there was nowhere for a suitable and designated room that are available for used, for training

Savate "the secret boots fighting art. In these times of barbarism, the masters showed the lessons for defense of survival to any prospective students, for

two kicks will be shown to incapacitate the target, or the three blows that will knock out an opponent cold: Techniques includes striking the temple, blowing the orb from the eye and cutting the tongue with a blow under the chin (Théophile Gautier, 1811-1872) "Le Maître de Chausson". 1842.

The oldest reference to this is that of Eugène-François Vidocq's memoirs, published in 1828, in which the author (see Picture 2) says that in the years of 1797-1798 "In the prison of Bicêtre, Vidocq was to wait several months for the transfer to the

Bagne in Brest to toil in the galleys. A fellow inmate taught him kicking techniques similar to savate, which was later to prove useful to him. An escape attempt on 3 October 1797 failed and precipitated his placement in a dungeon for eight days."

Vidocq was 22 years old:

Eugène François Vidocq (French: [vidɔk]; July 24, 1775 – May 11, 1857) was a French criminal and criminalist whose life story inspired several writers, including Victor Hugo (see Picture page 17) for the character of Jean Valjean (*Les Misérables*)

Picture 2 - *Eugène-François Vidocq. Mémoires. 1828*

" Beaumont wanted to give me a kicking lesson, and so we fight. And as I was dealing with a follower in this gymnastics exercise called savate, I was completely defeated. Nevertheless, I took my revenge in a shed where Beaumont, lacking space to deploy the resources of his art, was in his turn. My first mishap gave me the idea of being introduced to the secrets of this art and the famous Jean Goupil, the saint-Georges of Savate, who was with us at Bicêtre, was soon to account for the number of students who had to do the most Of honor ".

In the prison of Bicêtre, Vidocq was to wait several months for the transfer to the Bagne in Brest to toil in the galleys. A fellow inmate taught him the martial art of Savate, which was later to prove useful to him. An escape attempt on 3 October 1797 failed and precipitated his placement in a dungeon for eight days.

Le Malheureux Cloquemin Sous les Verroux, 1830, *shows a typical chain transport from Bicêtre to the Bagne.*

Finally, on 21 November, he was sent to Brest. As soon as he arrived, he had a stroke of luck. On 28 February 1798, he escaped dressed as a sailor. Only a few days later, he was apprehended due to a lack of papers, but the police did not recognize him as an escaped convict. He claimed to be Auguste Duval, and while officials checked this claim, he was put into a prison hospital. There he stole a nun's habit and escaped in disguise. In Cholet, he found a job as a cattle drover and, in this capacity, passed through Paris, Arras, Brussels, Ancer and finally Rotterdam, where he was shanghaied by the Dutch. After a short career as a privateer, he was arrested again and taken to Douai, where he was identified as Vidocq. He was transferred to the Bagne in Toulon, arriving on 29 August 1799. After a failed escape attempt, he escaped again on 6 March 1800 with the help of a prostitute.

If Vidocq is to be believed that there is a combat practice known as "Savate" before 1800, using the feet and fists (it cannot be practiced in small spaces and therefore uses large-scale movements) according to a Technique Developed (it is described as a true "Art" which requires an apprenticeship) taught by Masters (whose name Jean Goupil is an example).

However, according to Jean-François Loudcher, this date is highly questionable and it is very likely that Vidocq has heard of the post-Savate and then included in his memoirs. No other source refers to such a practice at that time.

Apart from the mention made in his memoirs, the oldest known references are an engraving of the museum dated from the beginning of the 19th century titled boxer from the quartier district and the dictionary of the low language or manners of speaking among the peoples of Charles-Louis D ' Hautel from 1808:

A little further, the author gives some details about the practice of his "Art" which further reinforces doubt, describing in reality an English boxing match and not a combat fight:

" one of them, BAS-Normand, known for his strength and his address, tried to dégoûter me from the profession, with the responsibility of public justice:

but he could be a thick lout against the pupil of the great goupy! The Bas-Normand died in one of the most memorable fights in the world, which had kept them from the dairy market. This triumph was all the more glorious, that I put a lot of moderation in my conduct and that I had agreed to fight only when it was no longer possible to do otherwise " [5] Amalgam is understandable because when his memoirs are published Savate and English boxing are still poorly differentiated in people's minds. English boxing has only been introduced in France on 1814, and although it seems to be known before, it does not include the public domain until the 1830s, it is thus mentioned and described in many plays, works Literature, magazines, press articles and engravings from this époque[6]. The few engravings from the beginning of the century, which represent the Savate, testify to the lack of awareness of the-gig theatre play. "The surprising gig-gig and the amazing Lamadou will fight for fighters as it runs daily in the streets of London, between people as it takes... Boxer, means in French to kick using a shoe" [8].

It is therefore more likely that it appeared at the beginning of the nineteenth century. If the savate seems to be known from the 1800-1810s in the popular media, as evidenced by the boxer from the quartier district and the dictionary of the low language or the manners of speaking among the peoples of Charles-Louis D ' Hautel (1808).) [10], it seems that les duels are actually spreading only from the 1820s. Several elements allow us to consider such a chronology as plausible to place the appearance and development of Savate Schools.

The first is the mention made by Théophile Gautier (Picture 1) in the master of slipper (1842) of a confrontation taking place at the tip of the isle of Notre-Dame near the red bridge (Picture. 3).

Picture 3 View of St. Louis Bridge. Between 1804 and 1811

Although it is not dated this scene, it takes place, in the 1820 s, because the former archdiocese of Notre-Dame De Paris was ransacked and burned during the February 1831 Riots:

" only a few years ago, when our lady was not yet a widow of her archdiocese, duels and tournaments took place at the tip of the isle, near that bridge called the red bridge (Picture 3) this deserted place was conducive to emptying the quarrels which ordinarily had the possession of some Hélène. The Champions were followed by their witnesses and asked before they started: "are we going to do anything". According to the seriousness of the offense appreciated by the latter, the answer was affirmative or negative. "We go from everything", it meant that one could eat his nose, if his eyes with a fork, tear his ears off, and use teeth and nails, otherwise, kicks and fists were only allowed, a difference that represents the first blood duels and duels. When we were going, the secret boots, the backstabbing, everything was good. In these times of barbarism of the masters showed the barriers, for two Kicks, the three blows: Striking the temple, blow the globe out of the eye and cut the tongue by a blow under the chin " .

The second is the absence, according to Jean-François Loudcher, of traces of duels with bare hands before 1826, as evidenced by the analysis of the police reports of the city of Paris. In fact, we find the first mention of Savate as a duel with bare hands in the gazette of the courts of 4 September 1826: "Let's sit down and say" Butcher Sit around the safe in the middle of the courtyard. Here it was about bare knuckle melee"

Finally the third is the date advanced by Joseph Charlemont in his work the art of French Boxing And Cane (1899) . According to him also known as Michel Casseux (1794-1869), the first savateur and the creator of Savate as a form of Martial arts. Michel dit Pisseux is son of a baker, and a baker himself. He was born in 1794 at the La Courtille sector, the roughest section of Paris, France. Pisseux is a baker and a street fighter. He learn many styles of street fighting techniques by attending the wine cellars, ball and cabarets around Paris. He added lightning fast kicks, unusual palm striking techniques and confusing shuffles that disorientated tough opponents, although small in stature he was the bully on the block.

Picture 4 - The Grand Châtelet of Paris. Around 1800. Sinister prison built in the 1800. The grand Châtelet was the main prison in Paris under the old regime.

Victor Marie Hugo ; 26 February 1802 – 22 May 1885) was a French poet, novelist, and dramatist of the Romantic movement. Hugo is considered to be one of the greatest and best-known French writers. Outside of France, his most famous works are the novels Les Misérables, 1862, and The Hunchback of Notre-Dame.

Woodburytype of Victor Hugo by Étienne Carjat, 1876

Bibliography.

1 Eugène François Vidocq. 's memoirs. 1828.

2 (a) Jean-François Loudcher. From duel to sword to duel with bare hands: conditions for the development of LA. Memory for the dea in education science, under the direction of g. Vigarello. 1987. (b) Jean-François Loudcher. History of slipper, slipper and French Boxing. 2000.

3 Boxer from the innocent neighborhood. Engraving of the musée museum. Early nineteenth century. The reference is due to j.- F. Loudcher.

4 Charles-Louis D ' Hautel. Dictionary of low language or manners of speaking among peoples. 1808. The reference is due to luc cerutti.

5 Eugène François Vidocq. Op. Cit.

6 (a) gig-gig, boxers, clown, alacte. Play in 3 Acts played on 15 June 1833 at the theatre of the dramatic follies of mm. Valory and st gervais. (b) Barthelhemy, lherie, léon de ceran. The Sword, the stick and the slipper, vaudeville in 4 Paintings, Paris, 1830. (C) Charivari, 19 September 1838, known! Known!, Napoleon of st. Hilaire. (D) Honoré de balzac. Splendors and misères of courtisanes. 1838. (E) Théophile Gautier. The Master of slipper. 1842. (F) Alexandre Dumas. Girls, lorettes and courtisanes. 1843. (G) Eugène Sue. The Mysteries of Paris. 1846. (H) caricature. 26 March 1843. (I) Trade Almanac. 1843. (J) Court Gazette. 10 January 1833. (K) Court Gazette. 2 February 1838. (L) Court Gazette. 7 January 1842. (M) Francisco Amoros. New Manual of physical education, gymnastics and morals. 1838. (n) Charivari. 11 December 1839. Lesson and advice, gavarni. (O) Agricol Perdiguier. Memoirs of a companion. 1855.

7 (a) Boxer from the innocent neighborhood. Engraving of the musée museum. Early nineteenth century. (b) Engraving of the ATP Museum. Prior to 1837.

8 GIG-gig, boxers, clown, alacte. Play in 3 Acts played on 15 June 1833 at the theatre of the dramatic follies of mm. Valory and st gervais.

9 Boxer from the innocent neighborhood. Engraving of the musée museum. Early nineteenth century.

10 Charles-Louis D ' Hautel. Op. Cit.

11 Théophile Gautier. Op. Cit.

Savate Master

Charles Charlemont (1862-1944) Series of photographic photographs devoted to the master taken by the agency roll between 1910 and 1931 (National Library of France)

Charles Charlemont

Charles Charlemont (1862-1944) was the son of Joseph Charlemont, he was born in Paris in 1862. He began studying savate and cane at his father's school. He showcased his first assaut in 1866 at age 4, at an assaut event organized by Louis Vigneron at Waux-Hall. He left school at age 15 to study wood sculpting, and then he was conscripted for a year in the French military service.

When he returned home from the army, he got back to teaching savate and cane at the gymnastics society L ' Future of the arrondissement.In particular, and at The Gymnasium Heiser 34 rue des martyrs around 1880, at the Lycée Janson de sailly and the artistic and literary circle in the 1890 s and at the collège rollin and the Lycée Condorcet from 1895.

The interior of the Savate Academy, 24 rue des martyrs.

In 1893 he succeeded his father at the French

Boxing Academy, 24 rue des martyrs in le district in Paris (this room will work until his death in 1944).

Charles Charlemont stands 1.66 meters tall and weighs 72.5 kg. He is described in the October 1899 Sports Journal issue, "as a man with the rock solid body , a chest like a wall, arms like columns and Iron pillars, and a strong athletic built." He will organize and participate in many fights, facing, Leclerc, Vigny, in 1896 he beat the Marseillais, described as one of the last followers of the pirouettements and the high game. In the continutité of the French boxers company created by his father in 1890, in 1897 he created a boxing company called "boxe Francaise" to promote French boxing through great public assauts. In October 1899, at the gymnasium in Paris, the press would promote a bout termed as "Combat of the century" that would challenge the English boxer Jerry Driscoll (English Navy Champion) to settle the supremacy of the two style of boxing, English boxing and French kick-boxing. Charles Charlemont won a contested victory, but he nevertheless assured the fame of French Boxing. In 1900 he became champion

Master Charles Charlemont leading a young woman in 1921

of the Savate amateur world against Victor Castérès. Charlemont will train many students and continue his family work until his death on 9 June 1944.

Picture Gallery of Savate Training

Young Boxers Maurice Castérès and Gerald Sulzbacher in French boxing under the eyes of Master Victor Castérès on March 2, 1905. Series of photographic shots taken by the agency roll (National Library of France)

La Salle Casteres in 1897. Master Victor Castérès (right of the image) and Eugène Photography From Universal Sport Illustrated on December 25, 1897. (National Library of France)

FUNDAMENTALS

When you understand a technique you know a technique, when you understand a concept you know a thousand technique.

Never discourage anyone who continually makes progress, no matter how slow – Plato

Experience is the most demanding teacher you will ever had.

On the next pages you will learn the fundamental target areas, moving, and striking techniques.

SAVATE

Was based on both physics and human anatomy. It has been proven during the Victorian era as the most practical form of self defense

Balance and Kicking Position

A state of equilibrium between all the antagonistic muscles which align our skeletal structure creates the balance essential to proper kicking. To develop muscular equilibrium relax elevate the knee and kick out straight. Suspending the foot briefly upon full extension. *Refer to the Photograph below:*

The Bound - Spring Principle

Spring or bound is the correct origin of all kicking motion, the greater downward force of the toe against the lesser opposite force in the ground produces an upward acceleration. The speed in which is determined by elastic strength in arch of the foot. Without spring kick, you lose both speed and power. *For illustration see the photo below:*

The Circle Principle

Circularity not only places an important role in the motion of the universe whether it be Sun, Moon, Planets or sub atomic particles. It also formed the essence of a well-executed kick. Curved motion requires the least amount of effort, which makes it structurally faster for kicking. Shortening the radius of curvature in any kick much like cracking a whip creates greater acceleration, while lengthening the radius imparts greater angular momentum. *Refer to the photograph below for your reference:*

Power Generation the Hip

The pelvis may be divided along 3 axis, the 1st is the x-axis that runs horizontally from one hip to the other.

Torque or the mass acceleration is increased by explosively around the axis is increased by

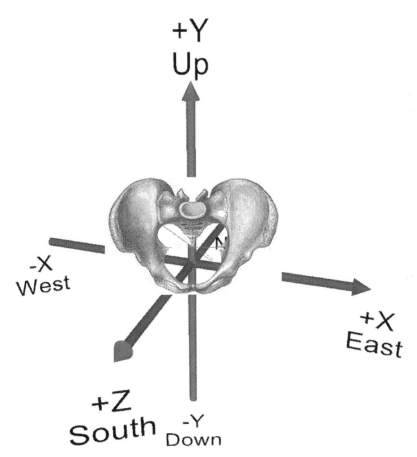

thrusting the hip explosively forward. The 2nd or the y axis runs vertically through the center of the pelvis. Rotating quickly around this axis creates power. The torso remains fixed and hips elastic and flexible. The 3rd is the z-axis, it runs centrally between both hips from stomach to back. Motion along this axis lends to the kick the added momentum of the remaining halves of the body. Hip thrust must be well timed with the spring to be effective. *See Photo for your reference.*

Of all the basic kicks the frontal chasse (Front kick) although appearing simple is often performed incorrectly. The weapon utilize is the heel of the foot in a straight position. To kick properly spring your knee up high thrust forward with the hip

extending the foot out straight. Keep your kick side shoulder back while leaning slightly forward at the waist to maintain balance. Do not kick target beyond the angle of the raised knee or swing the leg up causing undue pressure upon the knee joint.

Note: The kicking leg springs up in an arc, reaching the back of the thigh just prior to the hip thrust. Observe that there should be a whip like quality of the entire motion. A characteristic of a well-executed kick.

Against an opponent kick perpendicularly to his centerline. Kicking at any other angle would deflect the force of impact.

The Fouetté (Whip Kick) is thrown most effectively with knee leveled at peak elevation no later than the 135 degrees into the kicking arc of curvature, the weapons use are the toe of the shoe. To execute the kick spring the knee up 90 degrees into the kicking arc both take the hip inward bringing the foot around horizontally, then return along the same path, always twist your torso in an opposite direction to your leg momentum rotating the hip down quickly on its y axis upon impact, this relieves pressure on the knee. Note that the knee on the fixed leg is bent slightly and the ball of the grounded foot turns outward. The key to this kick lies in holding the hip

back where it joins the thigh while keeping the torso vertical.

The secret of a proper Chasse (Side kick) lies in the fluid change of direction in hip rotation from its Y to z – axis the weapon used should be the heel of the shoe. Spring the knee high and the thigh up perpendicular to the line of strike rotate the hip on its z-axis extending the foot heel out straight. Retract and down.

A direct line is formed as you side down your hip to your heel and out towards the target.

Relax the leg muscles allowing your bound and hip to do the work. The grounded foot should have pivoted 180 degrees with toes facing backward at the time of the full extension in compensation for the hips lateral thrust. It's important to avoid leaning the torso back or facing it down during any kick in that the force of gravity will reduce strike momentum. Chasse kicks are especially effective against all sections of the ribcage observe proper distancing don't allow your strike to become a push.

Target Areas

The fundamental ways of knocking out an opponent:

- Deliver a shock to the brain (example: strike the jaw or temple)

- Restrict breathing, limiting oxygen to the brain (example: strike the throat)

A knockout from a blow to the head generally occurs in two ways: by the powerful blow to the head which is the primary shock and by the concussion of the brain against the skull wall when the head suddenly rotates. See Figure A below for the target areas.

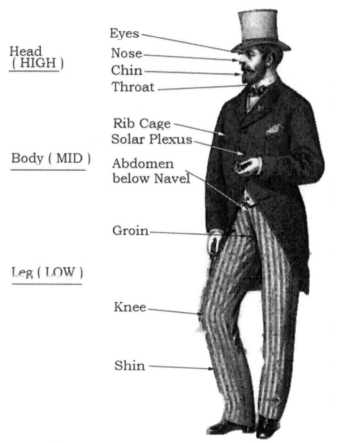

Figure A – Front Area Target points

For the Back area strike to the upper back impacts the lungs, heart, diaphragm, and spinal cord. This area is crowded with cardiac nerves that stimulate and inhibit cardiac function and are connected with the pulmonary plexus. A powerful blow to this area can force residual air out of the lungs, momentarily stopping the breath and triggering a spasm in the diaphragm as your opponent struggles to breathe. See Figure B below for target areas.

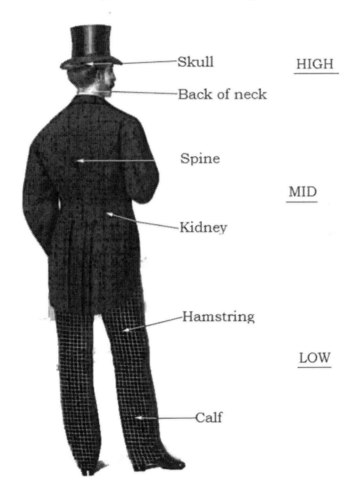

Figure B – Back Area Target points

The Guard

The Guard stance is the position we assume when in front of an opponent. The distance between the front and rear leg be the 19 inches or the distance of your shoulders plus 2 inches. And this stance should be of our advantage for both the offensive and defense against an adversary. It exist in Savate two guards: one false guard and the other the true guard.

The true guard is when both fighters stand in guard that mirrors each other. Say both the fighters stand in a southpaw guard position (left stance) or both fighters stand facing each other on an orthodox position (Right stance). To illustrate the true guard see figure 1 below.

Figure 1 True Guard

Notice from the illustration at Figure 1 that both fighters has both their left foot forward. Both fighters are in the southpaw stance. This is the True Guard.

The False guard is when one of the fighter is in a southpaw stance (left stance) and the other fighter is in an orthodox stance (right stance). To illustrate the False Guard see figure 2 below.

FALSE GUARD

Figure 2 False Guard

Notice that the fighter on your left is in a Southpaw stance (left stance). The fighter on the left has his left foot forward and left hand as the lead hand. While the Fighter on your right is in an orthodox stance (right stance). The Fighter on the right has his right leg forward as his lead, and his right hand as the lead hand. This is the False Guard.

If the guard in which you find yourself should prove unfavorable relative to the position of the opponent. Be it for an attack or any other combination. You can break position and walk without changing the guard.

The Guard is our beginning and end. With a strong stance, we will have strong offense and defense.

Walking

Advancing in the guard allows you to close the striking distance between you and your opponent. Leaving your opponent lest possible free space behind him, thus frustrating his movement and his defense.

Retreating in the guard creates gap in the striking range from the opponent and avoids his attacks and blows without recourse to block with the arms.

Distance of both fight is the distance of walking.

Foot work Drills

Mobility is the essence of fighting. To maximize the opportunity of an opening you need to be fast on your feet. A good footwork helps you evade all blows. Mobility in fighting is to seek your opponents opening or to avoid being the target.

Mobility in Savate like in many other combat arts is of utmost important. Since fighting is all above movements.

Moving Forward Shuffles – Allows you to cover large amount of ground in short amount of time. The on guard structure of the arm should be maintained, the forward shuffles involves the rear foot stepping up forward to meet up the heel of the lead foot(the front foot). Push off the rear leg and carry the lead foot forward. See Picture 5.

MOVING FORWARD SHUFFLE

Picture 5

Moving Backward Shuffles – This is the movement to disengage from any attack given by your opponent. To start the backward movement. Begin by sliding your front foot backward to the position of your rear foot. Then rapidly move your rear leg back maintaining the original distance between the front and rear foot. See Picture 6.

Picture 6

Moving to the Right – From your Guard stance step your right foot to your right approximately 6 inches. Quickly glide your rear leg to same direction approximately 6 inches to maintain the Guard stance. Note: When moving always move first the feet where you are moving to. If you are moving to your right. Move your right leg first. This is to maintain your guard position, and balance. See Picture 7 below.

MOVING TO THE RIGHT

Picture 7

Moving to the Left – When moving to the left direction. Move the Left leg first at approximately 6 inches to the left. Then glide your right leg to the left maintain the distance between the right and left leg from the Guard position. Maintain the balance while moving. See Picture 8 Note: Have a full body mirror in front of you when doing the footwork.

Picture 8

Kicking Techniques

1. *fouetté* (literally "whip", roundhouse kick making contact with the toe), Target are - high (haut), medium (médian) or low (bas)

2. *chassé* (side ("chassé lateral") piston-action kicking technique, high (haut), medium (médian) or low (bas)

3. *revers*, frontal or lateral ("reverse" or hooking kick) making contact with the sole of the shoe, high (Haut).

4. *coup de pied bas* ("low kick", a front or sweep kick to the shin making contact with the inner edge of the shoe, performed with a characteristic backwards lean) low only

Fouetté Bas (Low Whipping Kick) using the rear leg to strike the leg of the opponent. Fouetté means whip. Striking low line with the toe of the shoe.

Mechanics - The Fouetté Bas should be brought back a little quicker when you are not hitting something. Start the technique from the guard stance then pivot your lead and rear foot. Chamber your knee up as quickly as possible. And pivot your rear foot with the toes facing the back. The Fouetté Bas is best thrown with whipping approach targeting the low line. Hips turned out pointing to the target. A good pivot of the supporting foot will greatly enhance the power of your kick. You should be fast from beginning to end when doing the Fouetté Bas. (See Picture 9)

Note: When striking low line make sure to bend your rear supporting knee downward to achieve more power in Fouetté Bas.

Watch out for air kicking too much because it's bad for your knee joint if you snap it without resistant on the end. Once you developed the correct form. Practice the kick with a target pad, or kicking bag.

Picture 9 - Fouetté Bas

Classical Form Fouetté médian (Medium Whipping Kick) using the rear leg to target the body of the opponent. Fouetté means whip. Striking the body area with the toe of the shoe. Here the shoe is going to do the job

Mechanics - The Fouetté médian should be brought back a little quicker when you are not hitting something. Start the technique from the guard stance then pivot your lead and rear foot at the same time moving your arms up. Chamber your knee up as quickly as possible. And pivot your rear foot with the toes pointing to the back. The Fouetté médian is best thrown with whipping approach targeting the body of your opponent. Hips turned out pointing to the target. A good pivot of the supporting foot will greatly enhance the power of your kick. You should be fast from beginning to end when doing the Fouetté médian. (See Picture 10)

Note: When striking middle line make sure to straighten your supporting leg in order to achieve more power in your kick.

Watch out for air kicking too much because it's bad for your knee joint if you snap it without resistant on the end. Once you developed the correct form. Practice the kick with a target pad, or kicking bag.

Picture 10 – Classical Form Fouetté médian

Tips: The Classical form Fouetté médian gives you the advantage of a longer range of attack. While the Modern Form Fouetté médian provides you the advantage of your defense and protection. Refer to the next page for the Modern Form of Fouetté médian.

Modern Form Fouetté médian (Medium Whipping Kick) using the rear leg to target the body of the opponent. Fouetté means whip. Striking the body area with the toe of the shoe. Here the shoe is going to do the job

Mechanics - The Fouetté médian should be brought back a little quicker when you are not hitting something. Start the technique from the guard stance then pivot your lead and rear foot. Chamber your knee up as quickly as possible. And pivot your rear foot with the toes pointing to the back. The Fouetté médian is best thrown with whipping approach targeting the body of your opponent. Hips turned out pointing to the target. A good pivot of the supporting foot will greatly enhance the power of your kick. You should be fast from beginning to end when doing the Fouetté médian. (See Picture 11.a and Picture 11.b for reference)

Note: When striking middle line make sure to straighten your supporting leg in order to achieve more power in your kick

Picture 11.a Modern Form Fouetté médian

Picture 11.b

Classical Form Fouetté haut (High Whipping Kick) using the rear leg to target the head of the opponent. Fouetté means whip. Striking the head or chin with the toe of the shoe. Here the shoe is going to do the job.

Mechanics - The Fouetté haut should be brought back a little quicker when you are not hitting something. Start the technique from the guard stance then pivot your lead and rear foot at the same time moving your arms up. Chamber your knee up as quickly as possible. And pivot your rear foot with the toes pointing to the back. The Fouetté haut is best thrown with whipping approach targeting the head or chin of your opponent. Hips turned out pointing to the target. A good pivot of the supporting foot and the whipping of your kicking leg will greatly enhance the power of your kick. You should be fast from beginning to end when doing the Fouetté haut. And recover to the opposite Guard stance (See Picture 12)

Note: When striking high line make sure to straighten your supporting leg in order to achieve more power in your kick.

Picture 12 - Classical Form Fouetté haut

Modern Form Fouetté haut (High Whipping Kick) using the rear leg to target the head of the opponent. Fouetté means whip. Striking the head or chin with the toe of the shoe. Here the shoe is going to do the job.

Mechanics - The Fouetté haut should be brought back a little quicker when you are not hitting something. Start the technique from the guard stance then pivot your lead and rear foot. Chamber your knee up as quickly as possible. And pivot your rear foot with the toes pointing to the back. The Fouetté haut is best thrown with whipping approach targeting the head or chin of your opponent. Hips turned out pointing to the target. A good pivot of the supporting foot and the whipping of your kicking leg will greatly enhance the power of your kick. You should be fast from beginning to end when doing the Fouetté haut. And recover to the opposite Guard stance (See Picture 13)

Note: When striking high line make sure to straighten your supporting leg in order to achieve more power in your kick. The Modern Form Fouetté haut provides you the advantage of your defense and protection. With the arms guarding the head on the process of the kicking technique.

Picture 13 Modern Form Fouetté haut

Classical Form Fouetté Bas Jambe Avante (Low Whipping Kick) using the lead leg to strike the leg of the opponent. Fouetté means whip. Striking low line with the toe of the shoe.

Mechanics - The Lead Fouetté Bas should be brought back a little quicker when you are not hitting something. Start the technique from the guard stance. Chamber your knee up as quickly as possible. And pivot your rear foot with the toes facing the back. The Lead Fouetté Bas is best thrown with whipping approach targeting the low line. Hips turned out pointing to the target. A good pivot of the supporting foot will greatly enhance the power of your kick. You should be fast from beginning to end when doing the Lead Fouetté Bas. (See Picture 14)

Note: When striking low line make sure to bend your rear supporting knee downward to achieve more power in Lead Fouetté Bas.

The Lead Fouetté Bas can reach the target faster since your weapon is nearer the target than the Fouetté Bas coming from the rear. Once you developed the correct form. Practice the kick with a target pad, or kicking bag.

Picture 14 Lead Fouetté Bas

Classical Form Fouetté médian Jambe Avante (Medium Whipping Kick) using the lead leg to target the body of the opponent. Fouetté means whip. Striking the body area with the toe of the shoe. Here the shoe is going to do the job

Mechanics - The Lead Fouetté médian should be brought back a little quicker when you are not hitting something. Start the technique from the guard stance. Chamber your knee up as quickly as possible. And pivot your rear foot with the toes pointing to the back. The Lead Fouetté médian is best thrown with whipping approach targeting the body of your opponent. Hips turned out pointing to the target. A good pivot of the supporting foot will greatly enhance the power of your kick. You should be fast from beginning to end when doing the Lead Fouetté médian. (See Picture 15)

Note: When striking middle line make sure to straighten your supporting leg in order to achieve more power in your kick.

Watch out for air kicking too much because it's bad for your knee joint if you snap it without resistant on the end. Once you developed the correct form. Practice the kick with a target pad, or kicking bag.

Picture 15 Classical Form Lead Fouetté median

Modern Form Fouetté médian Jambe Avante (Medium Whipping Kick) using the lead leg to target the body of the opponent. Fouetté means whip. Striking the body area with the toe of the shoe. Here the shoe is going to do the job

Mechanics - The Lead Fouetté médian should be brought back a little quicker when you are not hitting something. Start the technique from the guard stance. Chamber your knee up as quickly as possible. And pivot your rear foot with the toes pointing to the back. The Fouetté médian is best thrown with whipping approach targeting the body of your opponent. Hips turned out pointing to the target. A good pivot of the supporting foot will greatly enhance the power of your kick. You should be fast from beginning to end when doing the Fouetté médian. (See Picture 16)

Note: When striking middle line make sure to straighten your supporting leg in order to achieve more power in your kick. The Modern Form Lead Fouetté médian provides you the advantage of your defense and protection. With the arms guarding the head on the process of the kicking technique.

Picture 16 Modern Form Lead Fouetté médian

Classical Form Fouetté haut Jambe Avante (High Whipping Kick) using the lead leg to target the head of the opponent. Fouetté means whip. Striking the head or chin with the toe of the shoe.

Mechanics - The Lead Fouetté haut should be brought back a little quicker when you are not hitting something. Start the technique from the guard stance then pivot rear foot at the same time moving your arms up. Chamber your knee up as quickly as possible. And pivot your rear foot with the toes pointing to the back. The Lead Fouetté haut is best thrown with whipping approach targeting the head or chin of your opponent. Hips turned out pointing to the target. A good pivot of the supporting foot and the whipping of your kicking leg will greatly enhance the power of your kick. You should be fast from beginning to end when doing the Fouetté haut. And recover to the Guard stance (See Picture 17)

Note: When striking high line make sure to straighten your supporting leg in order to achieve more power in your kick.

Picture 17 Classical Form Lead Fouetté haut

Modern Form Fouetté haut Jambe Avante (High Whipping Kick) using the lead leg to target the head of the opponent. Fouetté means whip. Striking the head or chin with the toe of the shoe.

Mechanics - The Lead Fouetté haut should be brought back a little quicker when you are not hitting something. Start the technique from the guard stance then pivot your rear foot. Chamber your knee up as quickly as possible. And pivot your rear foot with the toes pointing to the back. The Lead Fouetté haut is best thrown with whipping approach targeting the head or chin of your opponent. Hips turned out pointing to the target. A good pivot of the supporting foot and the whipping of your kicking leg will greatly enhance the power of your kick. You should be fast from beginning to end when doing the Fouetté haut. And recover to the Guard stance (See Picture 18)

Note: When striking high line make sure to straighten your supporting leg in order to achieve more power in your kick. The Modern Form Lead Fouetté haut provides you the advantage of your defense and protection. With the arms guarding the head on the process of the kicking technique.

Picture 18 Modern Form Lead Fouetté haut

Classical Form Chassé lateral Bas (side ("chassé lateral") piston-action kicking technique .It is a very efficient weapon in attack and aggressive defense due to its long reach.

Mechanics - The *Classical Form Chassé* Bas should be executed in one swift motion. For Beginners we will break down the movement. Let's begin in the Guard Stance .with your hands held up to cover your chin. Bring your rear leg up as high as you can with your knee pointing to the side, and pivot your lead supporting leg on the opposite direction facing the rear. This is essential for a great kick. Kick with the heel of the foot. (motion of the kick is like a piston of a car) It is important to bend the support leg when striking the low line and bend the kicking leg. Recoil or snap back to the chambered position.Settle back to the on Guard Position.(See Picture 19)

Picture 19 Classical Form Chassé lateral Bas

Modern Form Chassé lateral *Bas* (side ("chassé lateral") piston-action kicking technique .It is a very efficient weapon in attack and aggressive defense due to its long reach.

Mechanics - The *Modern Form Chassé Bas* should be executed in one swift motion. For Beginners we will break down the movement. Let's begin in the Guard Stance .with your hands held up to cover your chin. To begin the chasse lateral begin by flexing your knee into raising toward your chest with your boot facing the knee of your target , and pivot your lead supporting leg on the opposite direction facing the rear. This is essential for a great kick. Kick with the heel of the foot. (motion of the kick is like a piston of a car)It is important to bend the support leg when striking the low line and bend the kicking leg. Recoil or snap back to the chambered position.Settle back to the Guard Position.(See Picture 20)

Picture 20 Modern Form Chassé lateral Bas

Classical Form Chassé lateral médian (side ("chassé lateral") piston-action kicking technique .It is a very efficient weapon in attack and aggressive defense due to its long reach.

Mechanics - The *Classical Form Chassé* médian should be executed in one swift motion. For Beginners we will break down the movement. Let's begin in the Guard Stance .with your hands held up to cover your chin. Bring your rear leg up as high as you can with your knee pointing to the side, and pivot your lead supporting leg on the opposite direction facing the rear. This is essential for a great kick. Kick with the heel of the foot. (motion of the kick is like a piston of a car) It isimportant to straighten the support leg when striking the middle line and bend the kicking leg. Recoil or snap back to the chambered position.Settle back to the Guard Position.(See Picture 21)

Picture 21 Classical Form Chassé lateral médian

Modern Form Chassé lateral médian (side ("chassé lateral") piston-action kicking technique .It is a very efficient weapon in attack and aggressive defense due to its long reach.

Mechanics - The *Modern Form Chassé* médian should be executed in one swift motion. For Beginners we will break down the movement. Let's begin in the Guard Stance .with your hands held up to cover your chin. Bring your rear leg up as high as you can with your knee pointing to the side, and pivot your lead supporting leg on the opposite direction facing the rear. This is essential for a great kick. Kick with the heel of the foot. (motion of the kick is like a piston of a car) It is important to straighten the support leg when striking the middle line and bend the kicking leg. Recoil or snap back to the chambered position.Settle back to the Guard Position.(See Picture 22)

Note: When kicking you bounce and go back to your new Guard position.

Picture 22 Modern Form Chassé lateral médian

Classical Form Chassé lateral haut (side ("chassé lateral") piston-action kicking technique .It is a very efficient weapon in attack and aggressive defense due to its long reach.

Mechanics - The *Classical Form Chassé* haut should be executed in one swift motion. For Beginners we will break down the movement. Let's begin in the Guard Stance .with your hands held up to cover your chin. Bring your rear leg up as high as you can with your knee pointing to the side, and pivot your lead supporting leg on the opposite direction facing the rear. This is essential for a great kick. Kick with the heel of the foot. (motion of the kick is like a piston of a car) It isimportant to straighten the support leg when striking the high line and bend the kicking leg. Recoil or snap back to the chambered position.Settle back to the Guard Position.(See Picture 23)

Note: For *Classical Form Chassé lateral haut* the target is higher . For a good savateur who can kick high can kick low .

Picture 23 Classical Form Chassé lateral haut

Modern Form Chassé lateral haut (side ("chassé lateral") piston-action kicking technique .It is a very efficient weapon in attack and aggressive defense due to its long reach.

Mechanics - The *Modern Form Chassé* haut should be executed in one swift motion. For Beginners we will break down the movement. Let's begin in the Guard Stance .with your hands held up to cover your chin. Bring your rear leg up as high as you can with your knee pointing to the side, and pivot your lead supporting leg on the opposite direction facing the rear. This is essential for a great kick. Kick with the heel of the foot. (motion of the kick is like a piston of a car) It isimportant to straighten the support leg when striking the high line and bend the kicking leg. Recoil or snap back to the chambered position.Settle back to the Guard Position.(See Picture 24)

Note: For *Chassé lateral haut* the target is higher . For a good savateur who can kick high can kick low .

Picture 24 Modern Form Chassé lateral haut

Chassé lateral *Bas Jambe Avante* (side ("chassé lateral") piston-action kicking technique .It is a very efficient weapon in attack and aggressive defense due to its long reach.

Mechanics - The *Chassé Bas Jambe Avante* should be executed in one swift motion. For Beginners we will break down the movement. Let's begin in the Guard Stance .with your hands held up to cover your chin. To begin the chasse lateral begin by flexing your knee into raising toward your chest with your boot facing the knee of your target , and pivot your rear supporting leg on the opposite direction facing the rear. This is essential for a great kick. Kick with the heel of the foot. (motion of the kick is like a piston of a car)It is important to bend the support leg when striking the low line and bend the kicking leg. Recoil or snap back to the chambered position.Settle back to the Guard Position.(See Picture 25)

Note: Never look low line when you are going to strike the low line. For the lead kick the advantage is the weapon is near the target. Make sure you don't telegraph the kick.

Picture 25 Chassé lateral Bas Jambe Avante

Chassé lateral *médian Jambe Avante* (side ("chassé lateral") piston-action kicking technique .It is a very efficient weapon in attack and aggressive defense due to its long reach.

Mechanics - The *Chassé médian Jambe Avante* should be executed in one swift motion. For Beginners we will break down the movement. Let's begin in the Guard Stance .with your hands held up to cover your chin. To begin the chasse lateral begin by flexing your knee into raising toward your chest with your boot facing the knee of your target , and pivot your rear supporting leg on the opposite direction facing the rear. This is essential for a great kick. Kick with the heel of the foot. (motion of the kick is like a piston of a car)It is important to straighten the support leg when striking the middle line and bend the kicking leg. Recoil or snap back to the chambered position.Settle back to the Guard Position.(See Picture 26)

Note: Never look at the middle line when you are going to strike the body area. For the lead kick the advantage is the weapon is near the target. Make sure you don't telegraph the kick to take advantage of this technique.

Picture 26 Chassé lateral médian Jambe Avante

Chassé lateral *haut Jambe Avante* (side ("chassé lateral") piston-action kicking technique .It is a very efficient weapon in attack and aggressive defense due to its long reach.

Mechanics - The *Chassé haut Jambe Avante* should be executed in one swift motion. For Beginners we will break down the movement. Let's begin in the Guard Stance .with your hands held up to cover your chin. To begin the chasse lateral begin by flexing your knee into raising toward your chest with your boot facing the knee of your target , and pivot your rear supporting leg on the opposite direction facing the rear. This is essential for a great kick. Kick with the heel of the foot. (motion of the kick is like a piston of a car)It is important to straighten the support leg when striking the high line and bend the kicking leg. Recoil or snap back to the chambered position.Settle back to the Guard Position.(See Picture 27)

Note: For the lead kick the advantage is the weapon is near the target. Make sure you don't telegraph the kick to take advantage of this technique.

Picture 27 Chassé lateral haut Jambe Avante

Chassé frontal *médian Jambe Avante* [front heel kick("chassé frontal") piston-action kicking technique . The *Chassé* frontal *médian Jambe Avante is the simplest type of kicking technique in Savate and can be easily performed by a beginner. Chassé* frontal *médian Jambe Avante follows a natural movement like walking or marching.*

The *Chassé* frontal *médian Jambe Avante* is a kick executed by lifting the knee straight forward, while keeping the foot and shin either hanging freely or pulled to the hip, and then straightening the leg in front of the practitioner and striking the target area using the heel of the shoe. It is desirable to retract the leg immediately after delivering the kick, to avoid the opponent trying to grapple the leg and (unless a combination is in process) to return to stable fighting stance. (See Picture 28)

Picture 28 Chassé frontal médian Jambe Avante

Revers Lateral Groupe Haut (High Lateral reverse whipping Kick) using the lead leg to target the head of the opponent. Here the sole of the shoe is going to do the job

Mechanics - Revers Lateral Groupe Haut should be brought back a little quicker when you are not hitting something. Start the technique from the guard stance. Chamber your knee up as quickly as possible. And pivot your rear foot with the toes pointing to the back. Hips turned out pointing to the target. A good pivot of the supporting foot will greatly enhance the power of your kick. You should be fast from beginning to end when doing the Revers Lateral Groupe Haut make sure to straighten your supporting leg in order to achieve more power in your kick. Revers Lateral Groupe Haut looks like a *fouetté* in an opposite way. Using the flat of the shoe in a whipping movement. (See Picture 29)

Picture 29 Revers Lateral Groupe Haut

Coup pied Bas (low kick) from your Guard stance drag the kicking leg and strike with the inside of the kicking shoe and target the shin bone of your opponent. (This technique is efficient against a jab.) Note: Guard your face to avoid strike by your opponent with a round kick) See Picture 30.

Picture 30 Coup pied Bas

Punching Techniques

Direct Bras Avant (lead hand punch) the weight is on the rear leg or the front leg or 50-50 on both leg. It depends on the condition of the fight

You don't have to be an athlete to learn how to use your fists. You already have the weapons with which to protect yourself. All you have to do is learn to use them correctly.

It's strange but true that certain fundamental movements seem unnatural to the beginner in nearly every activity requiring close coordination between body and mind.

Fist-fighting is no exception. Some of the fundamental moves seem awkwardly unnatural when first tried. That's particularly true of the movements in explosive long-range straight punching

THERE ARE FOUR WAYS OF SETTING THE BODY-WEIGHT IN MOTION FOR PUNCHING: (1) falling forward; (2) springing forward; (3) whirling the shoulders by means of the powerful back muscles, assisted by shifting weight from one leg to the other, and (4) by surging upward, as in delivering uppercuts. Every punch combines at least two of those motion-methods.

Best of all the punches is the "stepping straight jolt," delivered with either fist from the "falling step." It has fall, spring and whirl.

You are not charging; you are being shot forward. You are not poking; you are exploding. A stepping straight punch to the head should land with the fist in an upright position to keep the punch straight. The instant you turn your fist to land palm-down in a head punch, you will begin to loop the punch. You'll learn all about looping later, when you study straight punches that are delivered from the shoulder whirl, without the step. Don't concern yourself now with balance and recovery. You are punching from the proper stance. As your feet, legs, and arms accustom themselves to the falling, power-line explosions, they will take care of your balance and recovery. They'll make certain that you still are in normal punching stance, whether you land on your target or whether you miss. (See Picture 31)

Picture 31 Direct Bras Avant

Direct bras Arriere (Cross) – Punch coming from the rear hand. The transfer of weight from your rear foot to the front foot. (See Picture 32)

Picture 32 Direct bras Arriere

There are three general classifications of "range":

> 1. LONG RANGE. That's the range for explosive sharp-shooting. It's the range at which most leading is done. At that range you're far enough from your opponent so that you can step in with a full-fledged straight punch or execute kicking techniques. It can be either a lead or a counter-punch. You've already learned that the falling step is used for launching your weight in long-range hitting.
>
> 2. MEDIUM RANGE. That's the range for rapid-fire, straight-punching exchanges. You are rarely at medium

range when not exchanging. At that range you have room to throw straight punches, but you lack the room to step. For those straight punches your weight is given motion principally by the shoulder whirl instead of by the falling step. If you're lucky, you may be able to develop a knockout straight punch from the shoulder whirl, BUT YOU'LL NEVER BE ABLE TO DEVELOP FROM THE SHOULDER WHIRL A STRAIGHT PUNCH THAT'S AS EXPLOSIVE AS THE LONG-RANGE, STEPPING BLOW.

3. SHORT RANGE. That's the head-to-head slugging range. You're at close quarters. You haven't room for straight punching. So you use Crouchet Bras Avant Ou Arriere (hooks) or Bras Avant ou Arriere (uppercuts). Hooks are powered by the shoulder whirl or by a combination of the whirl and upward surge. Uppercuts are powered chiefly by the upward surge. The hook is a legitimate shoulder-whirl blow, and it can be just as explosive as a long-range straight punch. However, hooks usually are more easily evaded than straight punches. Uppercuts also can be extremely explosive, if delivered correctly. And a genuine uppercut is difficult to evade. You, or anyone else,

should be able to hit harder with a hook or with an uppercut than with a medium-range, shoulder-whirl straight punch.

When you investigate the short-range blows, you'll learn why the ideal hook and the ideal uppercut would be delivered at such close quarters that stepping would be impossible. However, I'd guess that about one-third of all hooks and uppercuts are delivered with a step, in order to reach a target that can't be nailed by a straight punch. But the step usually is so short that it doesn't enfeeble the blow.

While we're considering ranges and their blows, let me stress one extremely important fundamental: A STRAIGHT LINE IS THE SHORTEST DISTANCE BETWEEN TWO POINTS. Either fist, in its normal punching position, has less distance to travel on a straight line to its target than on the curve of a hook or an uppercut.

Crouchet Bras Avant Ou Arriere (lead hand and rear hand hook punch) twist on the ball of your foot to get more power

A "hook" is a whirl-powered blow that is delivered while the elbow is sharply bent (Picture 33). Many people mistake a swing for a hook because each blow travels in a circular direction.

Picture 33 Crouchet Bras Avant Ou Arriere

There's a life-and-death difference between the two blows, however. That difference originates in the hook's sharply bent elbow. In the swing, the arm usually is fully extended.

Although a swing is the most natural blow for a fellow to use in self-defense, it is also the most treacherous blow that he can throw. The swinger leaves himself wide open to a punch from his opponent, both while he draws back to swing and while his fist is travelling in its long arc to the target.

Uppercut Bras Avant "uppercut" is a blow that shoots up straight (along an imaginary line from the floor) to an opponent's solar plexus or to his chin (Picture 34).

Because an uppercut rips up straight, it is very difficult to block or evade. It comes up inside the protections used against other blows-the guarding elbows, forearms and hands.

An uppercut's direction shoots straight up. THE HIP BENEATH THE STRIKING ARM SHIFTS OR FADES ASIDE. The hip fades aside to permit straight-up gangway for the fist and arm. It shifts aside somewhat as does the hip of a man driving a golf ball. And the upward surge of body-weight is somewhat similar to that in the completion of a golf swing

The right uppercut, however, is much more explosive from your normal stance than from the toes-even stance. Greater freedom for right leg-spring and left shoulder-wrench provides faster body-surge, despite the fact that the weight-shift from right to left foot is not as great as when the feet are even.

Picture 34 Uppercut Bras Avant

Uppercuts are particularly effective at close quarters against an opponent capable of blocking your various hooks to body and head or capable of bobbing under your hooks to head. The uppercuts explode inside his defenses against hooks. They shoot straight up into a bobber's face.

Note: As you practice those punches, keep your eyes wide open. Don't close your eyes as you step in. Focus your eyes on your target.

Picture 35

Defense

For our purposes "defense" means this: how to prevent a starting strike from landing on its target, and how to counter with a strike.

Strikes thrown at you by an opponent will include blows aimed for head or body with either hand. They can be swings, hooks, uppercuts, kicks or straight punches.

They can be prevented from landing on their targets by three methods: (1) COMPLETE EVASION of the blow by pulling away or sidestepping; (2) DEFLECTION of the blow by parrying (brushing away) with the hand, or by knifing with the forearm, or by shrugging off with the shoulder; (3) BLOCKING the blow solidly with the hand, forearm, elbow or shoulder.

Evasion is the preferred method. When you force an opponent to miss completely with a blow, he usually lurches off balance and leaves an opening for your counterpunch. Moreover, since the blow has not touched you, it has not off-balanced you for counterstriking. (See Picture 36)

Picture 36 Evasion

Deflection is next best; for the parry, glance or shrug usually off-balances your opponent without interfering with your own equilibrium. (See Picture 37)

Picture 37 Deflection

Blocking is the least desired; for a solid block not only affects your balance but it also may bruise the spot that makes blocking contact with your opponent's fist. Repeated bruising's of one spot-for example, the left shoulder muscles-can handicap your fighting ability especially when hit with a kick. (See Picture 38)

Picture 38 Blocking

Never close your eyes; no matter what kind of a kick or punch is coming at you, and no matter what kind of a punch you are throwing. Keep your eyes riveted on his left fist. After you develop the habit of watching punches, you'll discover that even though your eyes are focused on one threatening fist, you'll be noting from the corners of your eyes every other move your opponent is making.

The reason of giving you such a detailed education in the fundamentals of hitting before teaching you any defensive moves. Is for many reasons; but the principal reason was this: The best defense in fighting is an aggressive defense. Each defensive move must be accompanied by a counter-strike or be followed immediately by a counterpunch. And you cannot counter properly if you do not know how to strike.

That does not mean that 'a strong offense is the best defense.' That overworked quotation may apply to other activities; but it does not apply to fighting. It does not apply when you're pitted against an experienced opponent.

Another reason for learning striking first was this: You learned how to throw every important kicks and punch without having an opponent attempt to strike you.

It's wrong to try to teach beginners striking moves and defensive moves at the same time.

Most humans cannot have two attitudes toward one subject at one time. And a beginner can't have two attitudes toward fighting.

If you take any ten beginners and attempt to teach them striking and defense simultaneously, more than half of them will concentrate on defense instead of striking.

That's a natural inclination, for it is only human that a fellow doesn't like to get hit in the face-or in the body either, for that matter.

It follows that more than half the beginners will consider it more important to protect their own noses than to concentrate on learning how to belt the other guy in the nose. They'll develop 'defense complexes' that will stick with them. Fellows with defense complexes rarely develop into good strikers. Even when they are shown how to hit correctly, they sprout bad kicking and punching habits while concentrating on blocking, parrying, back-pedaling and the like. They 'pull' their punches; they side-step while trying to throw straight smashes; they move in with 'clutching' fists that seek to encircle their opponents for clinches; and they do much showy but purposeless footwork.

It's true that you haven't strike yet at a live target-at another fellow. Don't worry; there's plenty of time for that. And when you do start tossing at a live target, you'll know exactly how to toss. That exact knowledge will help you to become accurate and precise, as well as explosive, against a moving target.

Application of Techniques Illustrations

Revers Lateral Groupe Haut (Reverse hook kick to the head) with forward shuffles to close the striking range and reach the target. See Picture 39.a and 39.b for step by step application.

Picture 39.a

Picture 39.b

Tips: Quickly slide your rear leg and chamber the lead leg up with the knee up. And execute the revers lateral groupe haut. Striking the target with the flat sole of your shoe. Target areas are the temple and jaw.

Counter Attack with Fouetté médian *jambe avante*. After blocking the high kick you need to quickly counter with a lead fouetté médian before your opponent regain his balance. See Picture 40.a and 40.b

Picture 40.a

Picture 40.b

Tips: Strike the target with the toe of your shoe.

Chassé lateral *haut Jambe Avante* (side ("chassé lateral") piston-action kicking technique targeting the chin of your opponent. (See Picture 41.a and 41.b).

Picture 41.a

Picture 41.b

When you're in a normal striking position, RANGE IS THE DISTANCE BETWEEN YOUR RIGHT FIST AND YOUR NO. 1 TARGET: YOUR OPPONENT'S CHIN. Kicking the chin delivers a shock to the brain and can end the fight quickly.

The injuries that your opponent will suffer with the kick to chin will be a brain injury and/or broken jaw depending on the power of your kick. A blow to jaw can aggressively rattle the brain. The jaw is semi-circular bone that attaches to the skull at the temporomandibular joint. A person who is knocked unconscious, even briefly, or is dazed and confused has obviously had his brain rattled.

Fouetté haut Jambe Avante application. See Picture 42.a and 42.b

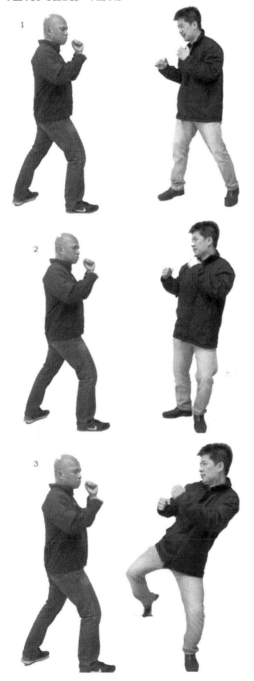

Picture 42.a

Picture 42.b

Tips: Hit the temple or the jaw of your opponent with toe of your shoe. Always snap or whip the kicking leg to have more power on the foutté.

Countering the revers lateral with Chassé lateral Bas (side ("chassé lateral") piston-action kicking technique. Evade the revers lateral then counter with Chassé lateral Bas as your opponent is recovering from the kick. (See Picture 43.a and 43.b)

Picture 43.a

Picture 43.b

Stopping a charging attack with Chassé lateral médian Jambe Avante. The Chassé lateral médian Jambe Avante should be quickly executed from a charging opponent from a distance. Execute the technique as quick as possible. Remember the chambering of the leg. The pivot of the rear foot and the hip rotation to deliver full power to your kick. The damage will be more devastating due to the incoming weight of the opponent. (See Picture 44)

Picture 44

Stopping a charging attack with Chassé frontal médian. The Chassé frontal médian should be quickly executed from a charging opponent from a distance. Execute the technique as quick as possible. Remember the chambering of the leg.. The damage will be more devastating due to the incoming weight of the opponent. (See Picture 45)

Picture 45

Direct Bras Avant application. Striking the chin. What you trained before will be applied here. Anything you use in a street fighting should be quick and powerful. You need to be very relax and control the situation. Don't show any fear on your face and be on top of the situation. The more relax you are the faster you get. Be quick on your footwork to take advantage to any opening. (See Picture 46)

Picture 46

Intermediate Training

Once you have familiarized the techniques you can now advance your technique by combining 3 or more foutté kicks without dropping your leg down. With this you can advance your strategy to giving one fake kick and strike the opening created. (See Picture 47)

Picture 47

Train with two techniques per training day. You need to be able to get the correct form first. The more times you practice a technique the more you will be able to be familiar with it.

Training has two objectives: (1) to condition your body for fighting, and (2) to improve your workmanship as a fighter.

THERE IS NO SUBSTITUTE FOR SPARRING. You must spar regularly and often to become a well-rounded Savateur, regardless of what other exercises you may take.

Sparring not only improves your skill, but it also conditions your body for fighting by forcing your muscles to become accustomed to the violent, broken movements that distinguish fighting from any other activity.

Much has been written about rhythm in fighting. Nearly every Savateur develops some rhythm to his movements in footwork, kicking, punching, etc. And some fancy Dans appear to have almost as much rhythm as a ballet dancer when they shadow-box. But when the chips are down, rhythm is destroyed. Your opponent's feints, leads, counters and defensive moves will break your rhythm in a hurry and will force your movements, on attack or defense, to be necessities of the split-second-to be violent and broken.

Because the movements in fighting are violent and broken, fighting is perhaps the most tiring of all human activities. A fellow may be a perfectly conditioned athlete for some other activity-like basketball, football, baseball, rodeo, riding, acrobatics, hurdling, wrestling, etc.-but if he hasn't had sparring practice, he will be completely exhausted by two or three minutes of fast fighting. His muscles will be unaccustomed to the movements, and he will be unaccustomed to breathing while making those movements and while being hit.

For a beginner, at least, Sparring is the most important conditioning activity.

Sparring also is the most important "sharpening" activity. It perfects your timing and judgment of distance in punching against a live and elusive target. It makes you adroit on defense and alert in countering. It grooms you to make exactly the right combination of moves in a split-second-instinctively

Shadow-boxing is the next best exercise for the twofold purpose of conditioning and sharpening. It might be described as fighting an imaginary opponent. It is particularly helpful in developing footwork. As you shadow-box, go through the same offensive and defensive movements you use in sparring. To be most valuable, your imaginary fighting should be done at top speed. Too many scrappers loaf at this work. Bag-punching is another exercise that conditions and sharpens.

GOOD EXERCISES FOR CONDITIONING THE BODY ARE ROADWORK, AND CALISTHENICS.

ROADWORK means running on the road. Running strengthens the legs and develops stamina. It also takes off weight if you wear warm, heavy garments while running. Regardless of other apparel, you must wear shoes that have sturdy soles and tops that come up over your ankles. Also, you should wear heavy socks to prevent your feet from becoming blistered.

CALISTHENICS for a fighter are exercises designed chiefly to build up protective muscles in his stomach and neck, and to make him supple. A fighter should avoid heavy exercises like weight-lifting, for they tend to make him muscle-bound.

After you've had six weeks or two months of preliminary, informal training-while learning kicking, punching and defense, and practicing them in sparring-you might adopt a schedule like this:

Shadow-Boxing	12 minutes
Sparring	10 minutes
Heavy Bag	10 minutes
Light Bag	10 minutes
Running	10 minutes
Calisthenics	10 minutes

The more you train, the more you enjoy the results.

Authors Photo Gallery

Andy Kunz in Spain

Kenneth Pua in Mt Zion Utah U.S.A

About the Authors

Kenneth Pua , has been in Martial Arts and Kickboxing for over 32 years , He started Training at age seven in the Korean kicking art of Tae kwon do (ITF) , Trained in Kyokushin Karate in Japan in 1996 and gained a 2nd degree Black Belt . Crossed trained in Muay Thai in Bangkok Thailand in 1997, and have fought in amateur Muay Thai Bouts (3 Fights and 3 wins) in Bangkok Thailand. He also traveled to Korea to train in Taekwondo with the best practitioners.

Kenneth also trained in Jeet Kune Do (Bruce Lee - Dan Inosanto - Paul Vunak - John Lopez lineage) and gained Instructor Level in Jeet Kune Do.

He is also the author of 3 Martial Arts books " KICKBOXING" , " Latter Stage Jeet kune do" and " Savate"

He is a Fighter Member, International Sports Karate Association (ISKA).

Fighter Member, World Kickboxing Federation Singapore and Philippines.

Semi PRO Fighter, Southeast ASIA's ISLAND INFERNO Master's Division Full Contact Kickboxing Champion.

Amateur Philippines Light Contact Master's Division Kickboxing National Champion sanctioned by WKF Philippines.

President, Savate Philippines

Kenneth is also a Professional Mechanical Engineer, Cinema, Theater and Acoustics Consultant, Audio and Visual Designer and is an owner of a Consultancy and Engineering Firm.

He Graduated with Bachelor of Science Degree in Mechanical Engineering at De La Salle University, Manila Philippines

Andy Kunz started his martial arts training at 9 years of age, He learned many different martial arts style. In his martial arts development he concentrated in Kung Fu. And hone his expertise in Kickboxing by training with Kung fu grand masters. He traveled to China and trained with Grand master Chiu Chi Ling (Hung Gar Kung Fu expert). Andy Kunz has competed in semi contact and traditional Karate bouts since he reached 18 years of age. The Bouts he participated includes events sanctioned by WAKO, WKA, and WIASKA.

He was Swiss, German and European Champion and won 3 gold medals at Arnold Schwarzenegger Classics in Columbus Ohio. He teaches Kickboxing in his Gyms and coached a roaster of fighters on weekends for amateur and professional Kickboxing Competition. Throughout his career as a Kickboxing Coach he created several amateur champions. He also traveled to United States to train with Dan Inosanto in the art of JKD. He is also author of 5 Martial Arts Books namely: Kickboxing", "Savate", Book of Masters 1 and 2, and The Latter Stage Jeet Kune Do.

Andy Kunz also worked as Chief Editor for the German Martial Arts and Kickboxing Magazine "Shogun ".

Ernie Yap Valenzuela is the official photographer of 3 Martial Arts Books. He had work for ARAMCO in Saudi Arabia as an Industrial Photographer. He is one of the most sought after still photographer for Philippines Cinemas and International Films shot in Philippines.

Savate Movie

Available in BLURAY, DVD and AMAZON

(Left to Right) Don "the Dragon" Wilson(10 time World Kickboxing Champion) , Andy Kunz, and Oliver Gruner (French World Kickboxing Champion and French Commando)

Oliver Gruner supports and promotes the Savate book and Promotes his Savate Film.

Savate is a 1995 martial arts western directed by Isaac Florentine and starring Olivier Gruner, promoted as the allegedly true story of the world's first kickboxer.

Synopsis of the Film " Savate "

1865. Joseph Charlegrand is a former French soldier whose best friend and comrade was murdered by an officer of the French Foreign Legion in Mexico. Looking for the murderer, Charlegrand is heading for a martial arts tournament in the United States because the murderer takes his pride in being a skilled fighter. On his way from Mexico to Texas some American rogues take him for a Yankee and ambush him. He can fight them off but loses his horse. On foot he runs out of water and eventually breaks down. Two young farmers (Ashley Laurence and Ian Ziering as *Mary* and *Cain Parker*) save his life.

When the farmers go to town for purchases they are molested and eventually seriously attacked by the roustabouts of a local business man who wants their land very badly. The film's protagonist returns the farmer's favor by applying his savate. Yet it is obvious they need further support.

Consequently he stays with them and even instructs Cain how to fight, so that he might win the martial arts tournament and hereby earn the money they need to pay the new taxes. But during one night masked riders burn their barn and one of them loses a precision dice. Cain recognizes this object, follows the culprit into town and confronts him. After Cain has been shot dead, all farmers are ready to sell out.

The hero decides he mustn't let that happen, hence he takes the dead farmer's place in the tournament and tells the farmers to bet all their money on him. In order to prevent him from being successful, his friend's murderer, the German-speaking *von Trotta* (Marc Singer) is hired. But the bad guys leave nothing to chance and also take Mary Parker as hostage. Charlegrand manages to cause enough confusion to disappear between two fights, so that he can free Mary and force Colonel Jones (James Brolin) to spill the beans. The alleged new taxes turn out to be a hoax but the farmer's savings are on Charlegrand and so they still need him to win the tournament. Therefore his final battle with *von Trotta* mustn't be postponed, even though Charlegrand has been shot in the course of action.

The French Foreign Legion had been founded in 1831, one year after the Garde Écossaise had been officially dissolved. Right from the beginning many German-speaking men joined the forces, often hiding behind false names. In 1861 Napoleon III used the Legion for the French intervention in Mexico. It lasted until 1867. At that time Charles Lecour had already created and established French boxing as a blend of savate and English boxing. Hitherto *savateurs* had used their hands mainly to block kicks or to fence with sticks (canne de combat) at the same time. One of Lecour's students was former army instructor Joseph Charlemont.

BARTITSU

Other Victorian Martial Arts that Incorporates Savate to their program is the English Martial Arts called Bartitsu. The Bartitsu martial arts was made popular by Sir Arthur

Conan Doyle in his fictional detective named Sherlock Holmes. Sherlock Holmes is well verse in a martial arts called Baritsu (is also Bartitsu) .

(Left – Illustrator Walter Stanley Paget is the reference for Sherlck Holmes , Right is the Illustrator of Sherlock Holmes Sidney Edward Paget)

Note : *Today, Sidney Paget is best known as the creator of the popular image of Sherlock Holmes from the original publication of Conan Doyle's stories in the Strand*

Magazine. He was inadvertently hired to illustrate The Adventures of Sherlock Holmes, a series of twelve short stories that ran from July 1891 through December 1892, when the publishers accidentally sent him the letter of commission rather than his younger brother, Walter Paget.

A Summarized History of BARTITSU

The physical base for Barton-Wright's revolution of the self defence milieu was his Bartitsu Club, more formally known as the Bartitsu Academy of Arms and Physical Culture, which was located at 67b Shaftesbury Avenue, in London's Soho district. In several respects, the Club seems to have been the first example of the modern commercial martial arts school in the Western world. It was a well-appointed establishment, according to journalist Mary Nugent, who interviewed Barton-Wright for Health and Strength magazine in 1901. Miss Nugent, who seems to have been quite taken with Barton-Wright, described the Club as "a huge subterranean hall, all glittering, white-tiled walls, and electric light, with 'champions' prowling around it like tigers."

These "champions" included an impressive roster of self-defense specialists gathered from around the world. From

Switzerland came Pierre Vigny, a highly experienced master-at-arms and innovator in self defence instruction, teaching the skills of la boxe Francaise (French kickboxing or savate) and his own idiosyncratic method of la canne (walking-stick fighting).

Pierre Vigny and his pupil Hubert demonstrating Bartitsu's Savate techniques

Pierre Vigny and his pupil Hubert demonstrating Bartitsu's cane techniques

Yukio Tani and Sadakazu Uyenishi introduced their students to the mysteries of jiujitsu. A Swiss all-in wrestler named Armand Cherpillod ran classes in Svingen (traditional Swiss wrestling). In addition to these worthies, the Club was home to a cabal of fencer/historians led by Egerton Castle and Captain Alfred Hutton, who were devoted to re-constructing the ancient arts of fencing with the rapier and dagger and two-handed sword, and who also taught stage fencing classes to some of London's acting elite.

Two other jiujitsuka, one of them Tani's older brother, had taught at the club for a short time during 1899, but returned to Japan after deciding that it was improper to promote their art through public exhibitions and prize fights.

Other than the arts of self defence, Barton-Wright's great passion lay in the field of electro-therapy. After being cured of an unidentified ailment by some electrotherapists in Berlin, he went to considerable expense in importing an impressive battery of electro-therapeutic devices such as the Nagelschmidt Apparatus, Ultra-Violet Ray Lamps, Light Baths and Thermo Penetration Machines. These and many other gadgets were duly installed in a clinic attached to the Bartitsu Club.

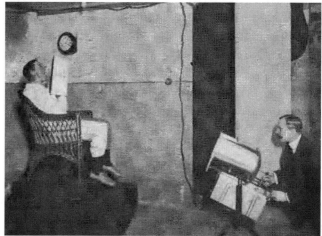

Light therapy aimed at a patient's throat to cure illness

The Light bath therapy Apparatus

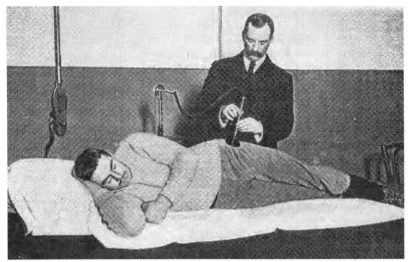
Thermo penetration machine massager

The Club was reported to have attracted a number of prominent Londoners as board members and as students. Notable amongst them was Sir Cosmo Duff Gordon, an Olympic fencer, who was later to receive some notoriety as one of the very few male passengers to have survived the sinking of the Titanic. It was alleged that he had bribed sailors in the lifeboats not to rescue others still in the sea, although his defense was that he was grateful to them and was trying to reward their courage. In happier times, though, he was to have been found learning the all-in style of wrestling from Armand Cherpillod on the mats of the Bartitsu Club.

Another notable affiliate was the prominent athlete and politician William Henry Grenfell, the First Baron Desborough. Grenfell was a fencer, big game hunter, mountaineer and rower, who served for some time as the president of the Bartitsu Club.

Military men were also well-represented in the Bartitsu Club membership, including Captain F.C. Laing of the 12th Bengal Lancers and Captains Stenson Cooke and F.H. Whittow of the London Rifle Brigade.

As well as classes for the general public, there was a certain amount of learning exchange between the instructors at the Club. Barton-Wright took it upon himself to teach boxing to Tani, although he later reported that the jiujitsuka had little aptitude for the sport. He also encouraged Tani and Uyenishi to coach Cherpillod in jiujitsu, in exchange for lessons in Swiss wrestling, so that they might all be better equipped to fight in freestyle challenge matches. Cherpillod was most impressed with jiujitsu but found that his Japanese colleagues were reticent about teaching him their more advanced tricks. He then adopted the tactic of feigning horror at their "barbaric" style, until one of the jiujitsuka agreed to simply wrestle with him in a freestyle match, which Cherpillod won. The learning exchange continued on a cautious basis, but Cherpillod knew that Tani and Uyenishi were still withholding their more advanced techniques from him.

Meanwhile, Barton-Wright and Pierre Vigny seem to have enjoyed a period of collaboration. Both men shared a similar self defence philosophy, and while Vigny was the younger man by about seven years, and Barton-Wright's employee, he was actually the more experienced self defence instructor. Vigny's walking stick combat system, as depicted by Barton-Wright in his magazine articles, seems to have come to incorporate some jiujitsu-based techniques, presumably due to his time spent teaching at the Bartitsu Club.

The Club itself was initially established on the model of a Victorian gentlemen's club, prospective members being voted on by a committee of prominent persons including

Colonel Sir George Malcolm Fox, formerly in charge of the British Army's physical training programme, and Captain Alfred Hutton, who also taught both modern and historical fencing at the Club. Once admitted, members of the Bartitsu Club were required to attend a series of private lessons before being allowed to join in the group classes. The latter were run according to a type of circuit training model, with small groups of students rotating between specialist instructors.

LATER YEARS

The last recorded major Bartitsu exhibition in London (during December of 1901) took place at St. James's Hall during December of 1901. The event started late and was then marred by unseemly public arguments about the arrangements made for refereeing a wrestling match as part of the display. Subsequently, during early and mid-1902, Barton-Wright and his instructors toured a series of exhibition events to venues including the Oxford Town Hall, Cambridge University and the Mechanics Institute Hall in Nottingham.

At some point during mid-1902, the Bartitsu Club closed its doors for the last time, under circumstances that remain somewhat mysterious. Subsequent speculation by jiujitsu instructor William Garrud held that the enrollment fee and tuition fees had been too high; it is also likely that Barton-Wright had simply over-estimated the number of wealthy Londoners who shared his passion for exotic self defence systems.

According to Barton-Wright's own report, recorded forty-eight years later when he was interviewed by Gunji Koizumi, B-W also had a falling-out with his "star" champion and instructor, Yukio Tani. Tani had been "troublesome" and had not been keeping appointments. When Barton-Wright proposed to dock his wages, Tani threatened him and the argument developed into a physical fight, which Barton-Wright claimed to have won. It is not known whether this parting of the ways was directly connected to the end of the brief Bartitsu Club era.

Armand Cherpillod returned to Switzerland, where he continued to work as a professional wrestler. He also became instrumental in introducing Jiujitsu, which he had learned from his fellow Bartitsu Club instructors, to Germany and other countries on the European continent. Tani, Uyenishi and Vigny all remained in London and established their own self defence schools, with the Japanese instructors focussing on jiujitsu while Vigny continued the tradition of eclecticism.

Tani made the best of it, by joining forces with an experienced show business promoter named William Bankier, a colourful character who had been a successful variety hall strongman under the name "Apollo, the Scottish Hercules." Bankier's shrewd management further established Tani as a star performer, a great novelty in the popular field of professional wrestling, and the fame of his jiujitsu continued to spread throughout England and then all of Europe.

Unfortunately for Barton-Wright, the new-found popularity of jiujitsu and then judo completely eclipsed that of Bartitsu, and in the self defence craze that followed between 1905 and 1914, he found himself on the sidelines of the movement that he had started. Although Barton-Wright continued with his work as a physical therapist, establishing a succession of clinics around London, he never again achieved the public prominence of his heyday between 1898 and 1902.

Barton-Wright had no formal medical training and, as the manager of a therapeutic institute, he was often viewed with suspicion by the medical establishment. His business was the subject of several lawsuits and bankruptcy proceedings during the first decades of the 20th century. With the advantage of a hundred years of hindsight, we can say that the therapies that he was promoting were of varying quality. Some, like the Ultra-

Violet Ray Lamp and the Thermo-Penetration Machine, were among the early ancestors of modern cosmetic and medical apparatus (the sun bed and diathermy machine, respectively). Other devices were of questionable value and some of them may actually have been quite harmful.

In any case, Barton-Wright persisted in this field for the rest of his career, eventually coming to specialise in the use of various heat and vibration treatments to alleviate the pain of rheumatism. By the time Gunji Koizumi tracked him down for an interview, in 1950, Barton-Wright was a spry elder of ninety years, full of old war stories and evidently still proud of his art of Bartitsu. Later that year, he was presented to the audience at a large Budokwai gathering in London; but sadly he was never really to receive the accolades owing to him as the true pioneer of the Japanese martial arts in the English-speaking world.

Edward William Barton-Wright died in 1951 and, according to the late martial art historian Richard Bowen, was buried in "a pauper's grave, because there was no money for a proper grave."

About Bartitsu Founder Edward William Barton-Wright

The founder of Bartitsu was born on November the 8th of the year 1860 in Bangalore, India. His name at birth was Edward William Wright. His mother, Jessie, was of Scottish descent and his Northumbrian father, William, was a prominent railway engineer. As Edward Wright was growing up he travelled to many different countries, receiving both a traditional education and a chance to explore various martial arts. In his early 30s he legally changed his name to Edward William Barton-Wright.

While working in Japan, Barton-Wright had studied two different jiujitsu ryu (schools): the Shinden-Fudo Ryu under sensei Terajima Kuniichiro in Kobe and Kodokan Jiujitsu, possibly with Kano Jigoro, in Tokyo.

By the time he returned to England from Japan in 1898, he was a man of the world, an enthusiastic entrepreneur ready to make his mark by combining all of the martial arts that he had been exposed to into a single, unified whole. Although initially focussing on jiujitsu, which had been exhibited once or twice before in England but never taught there, Barton-Wright's vision was broader than any one method:

Bartitsu's cultural origins can be traced to three primary popular trends of the 1890s. These include the media-fed panic concerning street violence, both "at home" and abroad; the public fascination with Asian (especially Japanese) culture, and the fad of Physical Culture and a means of developing both moral and corporal fitness.

Manufactured by Amazon.ca
Bolton, ON